TWELVE MAGICAL STAIRS TOWARDS SUCCESS

HARISH REDDY S

ISBN 979-888546767-4

I proudly dedicate this book to those

- *Who want to fuel their confidence and*
- *Let you know the importance of your existence,*
- *And the benefits of never giving up*
- *And also to choose a better idol for their goals and many others to create the best output of oneself.*

And also it is for those

- *Who is longing themselves towards success,*
- *For those who have low self-esteem,*
- *And don't even know the complete course of themselves*
- *And also not knowing the exact purpose of their existence.*

Because the author believes, one should start believing themselves by forgetting the negative assumptions of the rest.

Contents

Contents

Preface

The author chooses to write about success because we notice that we are inhabiting a modern world which subject to change in technology with the huge crowd of competitions to a one particular goal

And people are in a mentality that am I stand out to be 1st in that crew?

Can I win?

Look at those crowds of competitors, I feel never be equal to their talents.

These and other questions may have in folks mind, who has in thirst of success. But they don't know where to invest their time and energy to stand out to be first in the competitions.

The birth of this book is to guide the people who have a thirst in succeeding in their survival.

Here the author is self stimulated to guide his readers that before wanting the success, he is suggesting you to know exactly who you are, what is inner capabilities and how you can get into deep analysis of self course to get know your potentials to start your rightful journey towards the victory.

The entire content of this book is solely author concepts & understandings that can be put into action to get started with the practice.

Except author opinion, there are no other correspondents, friends, or public opinions that aren't judged to create a strong base for the author conveying's.

Read, realize and restart the progress from where you have been stuck to get ongoing...

Preface

The author chooses to write about success because we

Acknowledgements

Above all divine spirit of lord Ganesha, I'm blessed for being your forever devotee.

After three months of sleepless nights, I have been consumed to deliver this wonderful book.

This was the three months, I'm the only person who believed in myself on what I'm doing and my forever love and gratitude towards my parents who appreciate and believed in my solo success journey.

I honestly gratified to my parents for delivering me huge freedom to explore the world and now I'm very proudly acknowledging this book to my parents with promising words of I have been using the given freedom for my self-development purpose & pinning my goals on the focus list to practice on my customary formality.

And my great thankfulness to SHIVANI GUDEETI for being my forever constant supporter, motivator & appreciator for being who I am.

Acknowledgements

At the all divine spirit of Lord Ganesha. I am blessed for being

Prologue

First of all, I'm very thankful for having my book in your hands, and moreover, I appreciate your devotion to achieving your goals.

Thank you for believing, considering, and opting your hands for this book from the millions of books available out there and I hope your expectations of questions will be responded by my book.

Thank you

HAPPY READING!.

Author Biography

HARISH REDDY S

He is Professionally an MBA student, he found passionate about writing when he attained 20. and by self-choice & as a priority, he became an Author along with his professional career. He writes to influence/motivate & to guide his readers to be wise in knowing the world and to infuse positivity in society. **He became an Author for his first book "we are known to be unknown" (Which is about surface analysis of present human vitality)** He was very enthusiastic in writing and he is more obsessed with writing self-motivational content to realize one's self-worth & fictional love stories and as well quotes who inks in the **"YOUR QUOTE" app.**

CONNECT WITH HIM:

Instagram - author_harishreddy
Twitter - harishreddysss.
Mail Id - harishaarya1434@gmail.com

Success Intro

What could be a success so-called?

Is getting rich one day? Or being famous?

Success has no exact meaning or definition to conclude it.

Every individual & different age group of people have a different perspective towards success

and do you?

Of course, we believe, what we believe is right, right?

Let me share some phrases that I believe success is...

"Success" is something that we strive for day & night to get acknowledged by the world.

And success is not an end-stage that contains few stairs to proclaim your success, but it has endless stairs to keep going...

You're in a mind that you are striving for success, but the truth is you're just meeting your possibilities.

And Winning your every possibility is what is called success.

Success is not something that you label yourself by winning over your other person but defeating the old person in you.

Your success is assessed from where you were, to where you are now or who you were to who you are now.

Success is a book that contains the units which are named as possibilities & winning your every attempt of possibility is what called success.

ONE

A DAY WITH SELF

There are billions of people in this world and here I'm talking with you, about you!

Every Human (individual) in this world, has different senses, perceptions, and reflections right?

God made each individual should be different in one or another way because being the same there is no purpose in reality.

God uniquely carved every Individual and it's your commitment to knowing what you're fond to be.

Find that uniqueness in you

Find a way,

Balance Time,

Know that you're here to prioritize to achieve something, but not just........

Master the course of "self " in knowing who you are?

"MASTER THE COURSE OF SELF"

- **You're something**

That you should know,
Before letting others to describe you.

- **You're something**

  That you should choose your career,
  before letting others to shuffle your mind.

- **You're Something**

  That you should find the purpose of your existence,
  before your life gets departs.

- **You're Something**

  That World needs your knowledge & ideas
  before life assigns someone to express on behalf of you.

- **You're Something**

  That you can be your own brand,
  You don't need rich and poor comparisons.

- **You're Something**

  That you're enough to be you,
  You don't need any comparisons.

- **You're something**

  That you believe in,
  Keep going.

- **You're something**

  Your "Self" wants,

Don't Strive to become someone else.

- **You're something**

That you're striving for something,
Let the time decide who you're to the world.

- **You're something**

You know what education can give you,
And apart from that what you have to learn and implement on the go.

- **You're something**

You realize it's a solo trip life journey,
Realizing that living your Life is your accountability.

- **You're something**

You can become who you wanted to be,
By knowing where you have to start.

- **You're something**

That you can lead the world,
Not just live and go.

- **You're something**

You need someone to appreciate your progress,
Appreciate yourself, because only know your efforts.

You only know you can live, but your knowledge and talent (passion) hidden in you can make, shape, and can create a better world.

Be a person to lead. not just living to leave.

ÞÞÞ

A day with self is **"You With Yourself"**

Spending a day with yourself is like mapping an ideal path for a better longing for your odds.

Consuming a day with yourself will make you acknowledge your accountabilities that say no one is going to help to uplift you, but however, you with yourself can make you, praise you, heal you, judge you, appreciate you, realize you, and more particularly believe in you.

Because life is a one-time invitation in ***finding, creating, and meeting the person who you can be!***

Start giving rise to the person who you can be, other than who you are now!

Start Becoming the person where you want to see yourself in the future, not just how you want to look in present.

Reality is not a heaven, but hell in realizing the thug of your life.

Either it could be your parents, friends, relatives or anyone in your life,

Everyone will depart at a certain stage, some by faking and some by expiring, and in the end, it's you and your efforts in achieving something that will feed you to the rest.

"Believe in yourself"

Nowadays saying this word will never remove the dust in your ears to get into your mind and let you know what is the exact true power of "believing in oneself" maybe it could be a common phrase, but believe me it is the only base that takes you to place where you wished to be dreamed.

ᑭᑭᑭ

To spend a day with yourself just make sure you are away from everyone and from everything to acquire a space for some time to act with yourself. for better creation of your future, live in the present, not on your past, forget the people out there, just fell in deep conversation with yourself and ask these questions and find answers for your questions to get the real output of you.

1. WHAT I'M DOING RIGHT NOW? AND IS IT WORTH IT FOR ME?

Ask this question with yourself, and of course, every person has not lived in the same situations as you or like me. everyone is running in their life to acquire something.

Acquiring that something could be anything and what you are struggling to get is known by only YOU and conclude yourself where you stand.

Let it be your education, relationships, skills, and whatever other things continue.

command yourself, Am I pursuing my education at my best?

Are the relationships surrounded by me is better enough for my present and future?

Do I need to learn any skills or do I have any talent in me to start pursuing now to become something?

Just keep questioning and keep answering without any hesitation to know your "True Self"

2. AM I THE PERSON WHO I AM?

Am I the person who I am, or just pretending to be someone that everyone needs...?

Don't lose yourself just to impress the community, by forcefully don't hurt yourself just to "fit in" with the people who are "unfit to fit" in your life.

combine with the people who are of the same nature as you, if you can't find your niche then it's better to be alone and explore yourself to be better until you find your same niche people.

3. WHAT I CAN DO FOR MY BEST FUTURE " SELF "?

You have to choose your career, goals, and dreams that you wanted to achieve something, than before letting others to shuffle your mind and placing you somewhere with no way to exit.

4. WHAT IS THE PURPOSE OF MY EXISTENCE?

Am I existed for what?

The purpose of your existence is where your heart lacks you to survey the impossibilities & pour the possibilities to wrap that hole for a better base to the future accountability.

Know, whether you were born to change the fate of your family.

Or feeding the poor people,

Or to change the existence of our world.

Or Any other...

(and here author existence is all about feeding the poor, where he is in a moto to make our country "A Hunger-Free Country" he is relentlessly adding possible ways to make it happen)

There has to be a purpose of existence in each individual life.

If you cannot know the purpose of your existence, then you're a more disabled person from your mind than the person who is disabled in his body parts. And remember finding your purpose is not about making your life to a big living, but it should be all about where you have to lend your hand to uplift someone or a group of people.

Your purpose of existence is not about making your comforts, but making someone's life comfortable.

5. I HAVE TO SET SOME BOUNDARIES TO REACH MY GOALS.

There has to be set some boundaries to yourself or others, either you should not cross your limits with the people or people should not cross limits with you.

live in the edges of your life, to not to allow anyone to get your private life with a free ticket.

Keep it simple and healthy!

Don't be available so much to anyone.

Everyone will value more when you only available less to them.

6. I CANNOT ENJOY MY LIFE, BY ONLY CONTINUING MY GOALS.

Enjoying is not only just going out having a party, spending time and many others.

But enjoyment is also about enjoying your progress,

Appreciating yourself at each attempt by winning.

Enjoy the work that you do for your better future.

QUOTE

ꝐꝐꝐ

"GETTING TO KNOW WHO YOU ARE,

AND STARTING TO BELIEVE WHAT YOU CAN

IS THE FIRST AND FOREMOST WAY TO BACKPACK

YOURSELF TOWARDS THE SUCCESS".

- HARISH REDDY S

ꝐꝐꝐ

TWO

DEFEAT THE ENEMY IN "YOU"

Our brain is the best creation of god in our humans and it is our asset that is pre-installed in us and the rest is up to you, in upgrading or letting to spoil you with your negative thoughts, behavior, and attitude.

Your enemy is not your opponent or your haters, but a mind which always demotivates you and says you're not capable of doing what you're believed in.

Which is always filled with negativity, self-doubts, considering others' perception of you, not loving yourself, and Lying on others' negative comments and many others which don't fetch you anything but only depressions.

Don't you have a goal that you want to pursue and succeed in?

What is stopping you from doing?

Believe that this world can be changed for the better by only you.

Your mindset is everything,

How you act, how you perceive, how you dress, how you live, and how you going to leave the world. Everything is depended on how you assign yourself in your day-today activities. So make sure where you stand on your reflections.

Wake up your sleepy mind, which is perpetually striving for perfection in comparison in each person you meet. You're living in presence, not in fiction. Remember this.

Stop those idioms which say;

- I can't do,
- There are many others better than me and
- I'll never achieve Etc.

These words have power only when you assign the power to the words with your impossible mind.

believe me, Giving up on yourself and your dreams don't fetch you anything

You will never succeed because you have never tried.

It's ok if you don't succeed in your life, and also it's not about succeeding but trying.

Because at least your hard work towards what you wanted to accomplish, should inspire others to gear up themselves to pursue their mission too...

Because you may not be a successful person, but you will always be a successful idol for those who are inspired by your progress.

Don't get biased with what and all your mind assigns you to do. I hope you're getting what I mean to say.

Only you can control your brain to customize & appoint the task as you wanted.

No one is your biggest opponent than your negative mind and now it's your selection in either commanding it or getting used by it.

Your mind can be your best mentor when you take it under your control.

Some dilemmas will clarify how much you value yourself. Don't you know?

For example,

If you glance in the mirror & isolate yourself for a few instants, so now how you perceive yourself in the mirror, is what called "You".

It's all about how you accept yourself is matters, not the perceptions of the people around you or the world. so just stop concluding yourself that you're impossible for everything but possible for anything.

Stop caring about people's opinions and perceptions and forcing yourself to act according to that.

People's opinions are not permanent on you because they tend to change, When you change.

QUOTE

ᑭᑭᑭ

"YOUR MIND CAN BE

AN ASSET TO THE WORLD,

OR

IT CAN BE A LIABILITY

TO YOUR FAMILY".

- HARISH REDDY S

ᑭᑭᑭ

THREE
ANOTHER "YOU"

You always have another person in you, that you don't let the world know "You".

Don't You...?

Now it's time to have a forever meet with that person.

You have good and bad understandings of every situation, on every person, and on every living creature in this realm right? And you only express which is needed by whom.

Though you're concerned about the world, the inner "another you" is also concerned about him/herself before letting yourself care for others.

And you know being a human, it's our vitality.

You should allow your external one to unite with your internal one to see favorable and terrible things to add and deduct the decisions that you opt for.

Not only examining the possible course for your success but also knowing your complications in the journey of your success is what matters.

He/she is the only person "in you" who says when to act mature, when to be crazy, when to be rude, when to be selfish and many other things will let you know by the person who is "another you".

Squeeze you with yourself in everything you do...

Let it be your education, your skill station, or your passion, and whatever it continues. You have to invite the "self" to filter your thoughts, ideas, decisions & your progress to see good & bad perspectives in everything you do.

Be in partnership with the person who is in you & you, for a better realization of yourself, your life, and our world.

There has to be negativity in you, and nominating negativity in you doesn't mean you choose to splash the position of negativity. But it whispers that the reason for your negativity is to deal with the opposing people.

You should have a sleepy "selfish self" in you to choose to be selfless to donate and selfish to live your own existence too.

Remember you choose to play both the characters of you and know that when & where which character should permit to act.

The world is so much battling in hiring a good person like you. Because I believe in your selflessness to remake the world surviving.

And also better give a share of negativity to "another you" to vie with the people who come to stop you on your promising betterment.

Not being good is self-destruction & also not being bad is also an advantage to destruct you by others.

The world is not filled with only good humanity and again it is also not full of awful lineage. And you should not choose to play one role but you choose to build a personality of both decent and horrible quality to act according to that.

How to collaborate with "Another You"

Take a situation,

Review the things that hold your progress towards success than what approvals you.

Because finding trouble doesn't mean you're negative-minded, but a positive mind which always seeks all-around positivity in every situation by knowing the things which hold you back to a nonstop mission towards the journey of your success.

Review the things that hold you back. whether it could be a person, thing, or a situation whatever it can be pre-planning for your odds for a better smooth goo.

And that doesn't mean by doing this you won't get any problems, but even though before a problem arises you can expect the problem, and you will be free mind ready-made solutions and stress-free act.

QUOTE

ღღღ

"FITTING "YOU"

WITH YOURSELF IS LIKE

MENTORING YOURSELF

TO GUIDE YOU

AT EACH AND EVERY STEP

OF YOUR SUCCESS JOURNEY".

-- HARISH REDDY S

ღღღ

FOUR
PASSION

Passion is a commitment, a strong desire, and a strong emotion that you're getting started with what you believe in.

It is not a course to pay & learn but it is a priceless thing which inbuilt in you.

Knowing what you're more passionated about, it is a stage where you create yourself from "Nothing to Something".

Be daring enough to ask yourself what you're passionated about?

Each individual is passionated about one or the other thing, it is just that they have to find themselves in what they're enthusiastic about pursuing.

To find your passion

You no need to ask anyone,

You no need to get suggestions from anyone,

You no need to distinguish from anyone but the only thing is you have to ask yourself.

Being passionated about something is far better than getting skilled & certified in something.

- **Some are passionate about writing,**
- **Some are passionate about reading,**
- **Some are in singing, dancing & acting**
- **Some are in sports activities**
- **Some are in innovation and research activities.**

And many, in many strategies.

The progress is a solo trip, no one will force you to find your fascination,

No one will suggest you to do something other than your education.

Only you have to ***progress it to master it.***

It's ok whatever the value your passion has in this world, you have to pursue to name yourself something other than what your education has given to you.

Something you never get tired of doing, something you never get unbiased from stopping it.

Being passionated about something is not about conducting/or saying about your hobbies and, but yes your hobbies can turn into a hobby and that hobby can turn to be interest and your interest can turn into your Passion and your Passion can flip your situation, your thinking, your nature of living and choosing your career as your future and hooking yourself towards the game of competitions and constantly improving your Passion to land towards your success for flexible and deserved life.

Don't just keep on pursuing at one phase at only on your education and consuming over the rest of the time for your entertainment.

Those who are entertaining you are all those people who are practicing and acting to survive in their living and what about you? And of course, there has to be some dose of entertainment you need to laugh and cheer up but don't completely rely on that.

You too have a family, whom you have to feed them and they're doing their best to push you where and what you wanted to continue. and to the rest, they have hopes on you who believed in your future so don't disappoint them.

Don't pursue something by force of someone or someone who suggested this is best for you and without knowing you don't know where you stand in the end!

Choose your career! Why do others suggest you?

Why you don't know what is important for you?

Then research what and all-important and what can you do with that.

Learn to donate some time to involve, investigate and realize because doing this helps you to act mature and also choose your wise choices on a wide variety.

There has to be advanced and an alternative way,

you should choose, and choosing an alternative is all about finding and choosing your Passion.

Let the fight begin within you, and question yourself.

Am I fit to be only this I don't have any fascination with anything?

Just keep asking and there is no other way to get the profoundness of your existence by fighting you with yourself.

Your action towards your goals cannot result in a single attempt, but you have to attain an unlimited attempt to realize your mistakes, find better possible ways, and overall in shaping your inner personality.

Your Passion cannot be faked, it's your free asset.

Only the thing is you have to work hard to face many difficult challenges that are allot on your way.

Love what you do, Love the progress, love the improvements in you to stay focused on your Passion.

Believe that your mission which is full of efforts will bring you a lump sum of opportunities to create your way of living.

Are you Eger to find your Passion and to reach the address of your goals?

Then get set goo....

Utilize this III-3 stages formula to find your fondness.

1. **INVOLVE**
2. **INVESTIGATE &**
3. **INFILTRATE.**

1. STAGE ONE: INVOLVE

Dive into self-involvement without any distractions

And remember that your fascination is a part of your list of hobbies.

So you just have to make sure what and all your hobbies you are really habituated to?.

Don't add too much stuff to your hobbies list. Bring into the life of what are the hobbies you really love doing but don't just add what and all you like.

The thing is that when someone asks you what is your hobbies?.

You may have a long list to express, but the author is suggesting you just drag and list only the five best pursuits that you really habituated.

2. STAGE TWO: INVESTIGATE

Once you have the list of your hobbies, now the second stage is about investigating your selected hobbies.

How to investigate?.

Out of your five hobbies pick any one hobby, and investigation is all about what the hobby you have been picked up should put into action.

Whether your chosen pursuit is inbound or outbound it doesn't matter. Just put into action that's all the matter.

Just be in a moto of action towards your picked hobby for an hour.

In this one hour of time trying to pursue your picked hobby whether it could be writing, reading, playing, dancing, singing, and other innovative things which you think you are habituated.

And after an hour come to self-pace take a notebook and make a note of these questions and answer your heart out.

1. **How much joy do you get from your picked hobby?.**
2. **How much do you feel anxious to quit it before an hour to do some other task?**
3. **Did it make you feel energized?.**
4. **How do you feel about the all-around progress?**

Let you know that, the answers to the above questions should be honest and notable.

Remember that an hour of action towards your hobby you picked.

If it is made you tired & perhaps you wanted to continue after taking a dose of pause.

Rate your experience of your all-around experience of how you felt the feelings into percentages of pleasure, happiness, discomfort, and drowsiness, etc before your time laps for an hour.

And again for the next day pic, another hobby in the list of rest four hobbies & repeat the identical.

Be prominent enough to review your hobbies & try to give honest & deserved percentage of experience towards your action.

And also if it is made you tired, discomfort and forced yourself to quit.

Be okay with picking your next hobby and start investigating it on your next day.

3. STAGE THREE: INFILTRATE

And in the end, based on your investigations.

The person who distributed elevated percentage to his/ her hobby, and the other person who finally selected a hobby without any discomforts or getting forced to quit.

By the end of your investigation and infiltration of your hobbies.

You have been well involved and investigated the best output. And if anyone asks you what is your hobbies.

Just reply to them I don't have hobbies but an only hobby and that is this.

After taking the yield of your hobby, continue to invest a little time in it. On your everyday time. And that could be a journey of renovating your hobby into interest.

When it turns out to be interest, then you're one step ahead to name it "Passion".

I'm passionated about that & that was my hobby which is hidden in the list of my hobbies.

Once you name it as your passion, you will start making and finding directions to create a career with that.

Say no to people, who mumbles you're not for this.

You came so far because you recognized and believed in your passion.

You will achieve because I believe in you!.

It doesn't matter whatever your passion has a high value, low value, or no value in this world. You should continue to follow the purpose of your life and one or the other day Your purpose of achieving something will add plus value to your fondness.

QUOTE

ღღღ

"GOD ONLY

BLESS YOU WITH

A SEED OF TALENT(Passion)

AND THE

REST IS UP TO YOU

IN WATERING IT TO MAKE A TREE".

- HARISH REDDY S

ღღღ

FIVE

SELF IDOL

What how can I take myself as an inspiration when I'm nothing to this world?

Right now you may assume you're nothing but to become something you have to consider yourself in everything.

Self-inspiration is a pre-success self idol, that you can consider yourself to the best possible high.

Only you know who you are, what you can, and what you're capable of.

You have to honor yourself in everything you do. Let it be whatever the you're pursuing you have to admire yourself.

Dream that who you wanted to be, other than who you are now.

Take your "future you" as your present inspiration now.

There is no better idol inspiration person than wanting YOU, over others.

Choosing/making/considering someone as your inspiration will indirectly place yourself in 2nd role, by acknowledging/assessing your inspirational person should be first. because you have some manners of respect and love you have for them.

Though how much you accomplish, how much you are mean to this world, you always deem yourself 2nd by placing your idol as main.

So here the author is not convincing you, not to take someone as your idol but the author just recommending you that there is no better person than choosing you as your "self idol"

The moment you choose your **"future demo"** to fuel up your present journey towards victory is the best way to boost your life to a fruitful life.

Choosing you as a self idol can fetch better outputs than what you just expect.

Whether you achieved, failed, or delayed in whatever it can be. But at the end of each trial, you are at your best & first.

The proud moment is that when you are in the fame spotlight, where the whole world is cheering for your success, at that time there someone will ask you what made you come here? Who is your inspiration?

There you will be, you should superior enough to say;

In real who I'm today, was the demo I was taken when I was started to meet my "future self" to become who I'm today.

The answer is reasonable; I'm self-inspired.

- *There is no suggestions,*
- *There is no guidance &*
- *There is no command*

From anyone to become the soul of who I'm today!

It's totally my efforts, my failures, my corrections, my guidance, my motivation, my passion, and my realizations was made me stand myself here.

QUOTE

ღღღ

"BELIEVE YOU,

ACHIEVE YOU,

AND

LIVE YOU BEFORE

LIFE LEAVES TOU".

- HARISH REDDY S

ღღღ

SIX

NEVER WEIGH LESS

When you are at 1st stair of "A Day With Self".

The author said you're an antique piece of one in a billion.

I mean letting you the uniqueness of you.

When I say you're unique, even every soul who is surviving in this world is different in their residencies.

And when you attend the stage of comparison of a natural syndrome, you are slowly shading away from the realness of you, just to fit in to be like someone else.

Of course, you will intentionally bury your self-identity when you are striving to become someone else.

There is differentiation you needed with the people you live with within your surroundings.

Why comparison?

Isn't being you, is not enough for you?

Otherwise, you are comparing for what, to shine that you are high or to dull with you're not like someone whom you liked to be like them?

You compare yourself with others when you are not happy with your own existence of living.

Perpetually you are stimulated to get in comparison with the people of your neighbors, your colleagues and friends circle, your job, and your age group of people.

You weigh yourself less because you have expectations of there can be a chance of change to recreate a change in you to live like someone you like.

But do you think, you're fit to be managed over the role of someone on your entire living?.

Obviously No.

Because you tend to attract the attention of every new arrival to you.

Why do you want to compare your status of living with others' living?

You know living your own life is comfortable, but you cannot because you are uncomfortable in the impressions of someone's living life.

Be happy, be okay with what you have and only be focused enough to get what you wanted to achieve. And that's all the matter.

You cannot be condemned based on someone's good appearance, good living, Earning a good percentage of scores, on their happiness, based on someone's usage of materialistic things, and based on the number of friends they have.

It's okay whatever they have and live with.

Know that it's not your living, to mind about someone's living.

I mean to say, Just examine the different shades of people and never pick a shade that enables you to pick and install in you.

Because you already have an installed version of "self" in you, just upgrade that and let the real shine come from within you.

When you're in the state of comparison mind, either you degrade your opposite one or your own self.

Of course, the comparison is a natural syndrome in us, which is never get cured but can be subtracted.

We humans naturally tend to engage in comparison over the things like food, clothing, and choosing a job to apply for. And also you know that comparison leads to unhappiness.

Comparing things, money, personality and other materialistic things which you don't have, by comparing with the person who has that. This leads to unhappiness and self-degradation in you.

If you are investigating your perfection in someone's comparison. Where is your living?

It's, entirely, and perfectly okay with the way you look, the way your body structure, your fascination, your interests, and your picky choices, and many others.

That's cool actually, you are living the way you are, the way you wanted to be.

Never try to accumulate different shades of lineage in you by striving with comparisons.

Build confidence in yourself that, you may not be better than someone, but know that you have no reason to compare yourself with anyone else.

You cannot be always better than everyone else and also you cannot be lesser than anyone else.

It's you, you were born to be you, you are growing to be the way you are, and living the way you wanted to be.

Never be a slave for comparison to weigh you less or more in front of others.

If you think you're better, there are people who are better than you.

If you think you are ugly, there will be somebody who is uglier than you.

It's just you and you, and that's all the matter of your own living.

NEVER WEIGH YOURSELF LESS IN FRONT OF ANYONE ELSE.

QUOTE

ღღღ

"COMPARING YOURSELF

WITH OTHERS IS LIKE

MAKING YOURSELF DEAD

AND REMEMBERING SOMEONE ELSE

IN YOUR PLACE AND THINKING

THAT'S YOU".

It's Entirely Worthless.

- HARISH REDDY S

ღღღ

SEVEN

WHY WORRY?, BE HAPPY!

Why you worried?

Do you feel no one is there to assist you with the considerable possible ways to your progress?

Or

Do you feel no one is comfortable with what you're pursuing?

It's okay! You're almost equal to the whole galaxy. I completely believe in you and you don't need the above people to add to your success club.

Of course, no one will gonna help you,

Of course, you have many friends and relatives though they exists to congratulate you but no one will come in to look into your progress to correct you and guide you.

It's all your efforts and results that you have to invest and get it.

In fact, more I can say that everyone is busy with leading their own lives.

They have no time to look after you, to guide you. Only you have chosen to believe what you choose to achieve.

And there is no turning your head into 360 degrees to look back to see who is coming to help you. But believe no one will.

- **Some will be happy with you,**
- **Some hate you,**
- **Some will get jealous of you and**
- **Some will never care about you!.**

You are living with these behaviors, which are surrounded by you. But choose

- **Which has to be kept,**
- **Which has to be observed and**
- **Which category of people has to be thrown out of your life.**

The time you live and achieve is more precious than being get influenced by the negative people to trap you into the deep down of negative seashore.

People are intended to appreciate you on your first win, and observe you to the rest of your further actions.

We, humans, are flourished with the tendency of we always focusing on that one person who hates us by leaving the 99% of people who love us.

And it's okay if the above statement is the opposite in your life, but be happy because you have to get focused on that one person appreciation than the rest of 99% of haters.

There are some people in your life to appreciate you and be flexible enough to get motivated with small appreciations.

You're worried because you are concerned and expecting happiness from the people who are not even happy with your progress. Don't stay there anymore, because you're expecting to fall rainy happiness on you, by locking and occupying yourself within the room of negative people, come out and see there will be few people who are spreading the news of your success to the whole world, better be happy with them and get soo tired in spending time with those people that you don't even have the time to look /hear what the world is thinking about you.

Be happy because even the whole world is not happy or not even recognizing your talent, your parents are always happy and say that my daughter made this or my son wrote this, if Your parents are happy with what you are doing, then never stop continuing to not get acknowledged by the world, but by your parents.

Focus on where you are valued, being inspired by you, and being appreciated for being you. Stick there and believe that is your whole world and continue to pursue to proclaim the things of your next opportunities.

QUOTE

ღღღ

"FOCUS ON YOUR

EXISTENCE,

NOT ON YOUR

SURROUNDINGS".

- HARISH REDDY S

ღღღ

EIGHT

BE RESPONSIBLE

Of course, you should!

You have to be Responsible & a caretaker of your goals.

How you're being responsible in taking care of yourself from accidents, negativity, and many other things to live your life at your fullest. in the same way you have to be Responsible for continuing your goals.

Don't you know?

You're worth enough than just living, and great enough to place yourself in a high position by only being responsible & Not giving up attitude.

Pursuing your goals is not just like doing according to your mood swings, it has to be having some prioritized time, self-involvement & above all being responsible to continue on your daily routine without skipping.

You have to set a time at your self-involvement pace & pin it for a daily routine.

Don't be just like being interested in doing today and denying after a few days.

You're Denying For What?

Is because you're not getting time?

Or are you feel like giving up?

Or do you feel unfit to pursue?

Or are you feeling about how others think of you?

It's okay! these questions are just a small bridge that takes a very long time in shaping your personality, building your confidence & making you realize you are the best, and more particularly it will let you know the significance of time.

No successful men/women who are never occupied by success without crossing this small bridge and taking a long time is all about how you accept the people's actions and occupy yourself in reality.

The world has many ways to entertain you, by means in more possible ways but besides it is up to you in building your future or spoiling it.

Take your entertainment time as a lease for building your future best life.

And know that whenever you are stuck in your development.

Use this "R^{-3}" formula to set back right and to move straight ahead.

The R^{-3} Is...

- **REVIEW**
- **REALISE &**
- **RESTART**

1. REVIEW:

If you feel like you're stuck in your progress, or something which is making you lose interest in doing, or something which is demotivating you.

Make an Analysis of these to the output of what is exactly holding you.

2. REALISE:

After reviewing your questions.

Realize that what has been stopped you.

Whether it could be an enemy in you, or a situation, or a person. Never allow any negativity to get into your mind and spoil you entirely. Just remove whatever things that hold you back on a smooth goo towards your goals

3. RESTART:

Come on. You have been already cleared your direction by removing the things which holded you back.

When you're at the phase of **Review** by diving into it you may have gotten certain people, things, and situations into your mind that don't weigh any existence in your life.

Whoever the people, whatever the situation or things you felt when you're at the phase of **Reviewing** are the only things that manipulate you back. And now it is the time to clear those uncleared caches from your energy.

So here I'm very concerned about you in saying that:

You're the only person who is responsible for your achievements, mistakes, and disappointments so just don't make excuses in opposing on someone else.

QUOTE

ღღღ

"YOU DESERVED TO

GET ACKNOWLEDGED

TOWARDS WHAT YOU

ARE BEING RESPONSIBLE".

- HARISH REDDY S

ღღღ

NINE

NO MOTIVATION

You don't require motivation.

What?

Of course, you don't need to crave that.

Getting/Wanting motivation is all about forcing yourself unwantedly towards the things you want.

Seriously if you are really persistent towards motivation, you will never grow as a high person in these billions of crew.

Someone should not come to push and instruct you to resume the work that you have been paused.

In fact, you're consuming the motivation for what?

To Force yourself? Or

To Convince yourself?

If you are really determined to push yourself by force, then hold a second and quiet the journey.

Because once you lose motivation you lose yourself, your time, your efforts, and your energy.

And that's the stage that we call Failure!

You ceased to function further because you lose the motivation in you just because you habituated with that.

Only the person who has well-forecasted plans for his/her forthcoming future are the only people who are committed to success to succeed for sure.

There is a formula that I believe may stimulate you for being methodical than just being motivated.

The Formula is **S-H-I-F-T**

It is named as a shift for easy memory but actually, it has a procedure to go step by step.

1. **TIME**
2. **SCHEDULE**
3. **HEALTH**
4. **FORECAST AND**
5. **INSTALL**

Let's dive into **FIRST STAGE:**

1. TIME

Time is the most expensive thing when you get to know the value of time!.

You should have the commitment to get done with that stuff which is dragging you to do tomorrow, tomorrow, and some other day will lead to no time to do on any day.

I just want to convey the value of you and the time that you invest in your goals.

- **Take time to believe in yourself.**
- **Take time to build confidence in yourself.**
- **Take time to build a strong base on what you believed in (Your passion or goals)**
- **Take time to know your "own self".**
- **Take time to assess your do's and don'ts that allots on your future journey.**

Just take time, let it take days, weeks, months, or years. No problem.

Because it's your base, so fill it properly with no holes to not allow negativity to get fit in.

Inspect your own self to be flexible to adjust with your future creation.

Remember it's a solo review again you don't need the motivation to evaluate.

2. SCHEDULE

Have a far scope of 5 or 10 years based on the goals you expected to achieve.

Organize your goals on your daily, weekly, monthly, and yearly and review the results based on each attempt.

Remember establishing your future is not big deal but make sure you're existing enough to stay on track.

Be confident with scheduling and Be prominent with proceeding.

3. FORECAST

Predict the future based on your schedule. It may not be 100% prediction but it's way better than staying dumb right?

Predict it like what I could be after years if I do this now?

Ever remember that you have to forecast your future life based on your existence, your family, and your essence of living.

Because these are the things which you got biased and grown up with.

Proceed now, There is no better day than starting it today.

4. HEALTH

Your health has a lot of impact on your existence and continued survival and on your happy smile.

Focus on your health.

5. INSTALL

Now install the program of the forecasted program of your future to **SHIFT** from "Need Motivation" to "No Motivation"

For effective success name your goals as "Responsibilities" not just goals as "Goals".

QUOTE

ჯჯჯ

"YOU DON'T NEED MOTIVATION

YOU JUST NEED A PROPER METHOD

TO PURSUE YOUR GOALS"

- HARISH REDDY S

ჯჯჯ

TEN

END FRUIT.

You notice that people are biased in judging a person on their behavior, their progress, and their results.

Whether you could be whatever the thing you are pursuing people tend to judge you. Indirectly they say where you stand on something is not fruitful for you, instead of that they show you that is best, this is best, that has future, and this has future, etc etc etc. And of course few people you may have in your life, to suggest you and guide you. And that's a great thing.

Okay, let's dip into the chapter.

Do You know what is end fruit?

It says that whatever the stuff you are continuing it could be your education, skills, passion, or your goals and dreams, oh god there are many professions and these are pursued by the people who are passionated in a particular domain.

And you are following that because you perceive what you will learn from that, you understand what you will be going to gain after completing your persuasion.

You're doing something because, you know that will going to be plus value to your income, your reputation, and/

or for your entire possession.

And now I can ask you, what you're doing right at present, has an end space to seize your recognitions?

Maybe I believe possibly your answer could be the "YES"

Because I assume that no individual will ever debit their money, time, and hard work if there is no output of credits for their efforts.

And if you are don't know the end fruit of your persuasion.

Right now I request you to start forecasting by your present stand and ask yourself what I wanted to get by doing this?

Just dig the journey of your past efforts, present persuasion & also to forecast your future.

Try to know that what you are doing right now? And what you are going to get in the end?

When you speak about your education process, goals or jobs, or any additional things with the public domain of your surroundings.

- People start to Suggest you.
- Some people will guide you.
- Some people will warn you.
- Some people will bully you and
- Some other people will never care about you.

Now just whatever you receive from the above phrases Just take the suggestions and

- Research with the people who guided you,
- Know the drawbacks of the people who warned you.
- Calm and forget about the people who bullied you and

- Never even exists to live the lives of The people who never cared about your validity.

Whatever the shuffled collections you get it from the different sources of people. Involve, investigate and interpret & arrive at the best output of possible remedies.

Ultimately in the billions of world, you are an antique piece in knowing the end credit of your current progress.

It's your obligation in leading your own life, no parents, no friends, and no relatives which you blindly speculate they're there for you.

But it's absolutely none of them, they only exists to give you free advice and guidance but only you to make and utilize it perfectly for a strong base for your future.

Your end fruit can be predicted based on the performance you put on your daily basis to get it.

End fruit is like watering a small plant of hopes and taking care of your plant by manuring with confidence to forecast to get the best fruit after years.

In the same path, how you choose your goals, adopting the right strategies with consistency to proclaim your success by your best.

Because it is solely your life, don't lend it to someone else to predict an unentertained future for you.

Whatever you're supposed in doing,

Never stop, focus only on the improvements in you, not on your endeavors.

- Keep learning,
- Keep going,
- Keep improving and
- Keep achieving.

QUOTE

♡♡♡

"KNOW THAT,

BELIEVE THAT,

ACT THAT,

MAKE THAT AND

LIVE WITH THAT".

- HARISH REDDY S

♡♡♡

ELEVEN

PROCLAIM AT EACH STAIR.

Discover the enjoyment of your life.

Learn to rejoice in your victory.

Whatever you have been achieved, have been achieving, and what you going to achieve.

Never deny making a freeze of time to celebrate your Victory.

It's okay what's the weight/value of your victory.

Never quit celebrating each attempt of success.

And by means, it is your biggest happiness for you, because you know the hard work behind the success is you're enjoying today.

And that's the thing, even I want to celebrate your win.

Know that being celebrated your every attempt of accomplishment, is your biggest, strongest and boldest self-appraisal that you ever tag yourself to give a better try to the next attempt.

Celebrate it.

There are no comparison findings of your victory with other person capabilities.

What you achieved, is by your capabilities and what you going to achieve is about how you manure your skills.

If you are happy with your results and trials that's all that I can convey or suggest to you.

Make a circle of living with the people, who are positively influenced, those who are with good vibes, and those who spread good smiles everywhere.

If you are satisfied with what you have, there is the entry of true happiness that you can live with

QUOTE

ᑭᑭᑭ

"THERE IS AN ENTRY OF TRUE HAPPINESS,

WHEN THERE IS NO COMPARISON

OR JEALOUS OF OTHERS' WINNING".

- HARISH REDDY S

ᑭᑭᑭ

TWELVE
KEEP GOING

When you're completely done with investing your time and coming up climbing till the eleventh stair.

And this 12th stair is not a determination to conclude but a start of your beginning.

The whole Elven stairs is a course about filling the emptiness in you, to let you know who you are.

And this 12th notch is a stage where you are ready to fight with the world.

You're equal to the whole universe and never feel alone to battle with the world of thrones.

1. **A DAY WITH SELF**: You understand who you are.
2. **DEFEAT THE ENEMY IN YOU**: You have been taking control of your mind.
3. **ANOTHER YOU:** You met the person who is in you.
4. **PASSION:** Your passion should be defined by your name. Never stop until.
5. **SELF IDOL:** Your inspiration is you.
6. **NEVER WEIGH LESS**: You're just the way you are. You are God's creation and you're real. let the realness shine.

7. **WHY WORRY?, BE HAPPY!:** In the end, the happiness was created by you, not the rest.
8. **BE RESPONSIBLE:** Grow mature, and be responsible towards your goal.
9. **NO MOTIVATION:** Regulate the track, towards your goals.
10. **END FRUIT:** Only you know the present struggle to touch your end shine
11. **PROCLAIM AT EACH STAIR:** Celebrate it, when you have been given your best.
12. **KEEP GOING:** Be on-trend, to trend with the trendings.

The world has many opponents and we don't know who will deny at what stage.

And I believe you will never deny because you got to know, who you are, what's your purpose and what is the responsibility of your existence.

Just keep Going...

QUOTE

ÞÞÞ

"THERE IS NO END SHUTDOWN

BUT

A PROGRESS TO KEEP YOU FOCUSED"

- HARISH REDDY S

ÞÞÞ

Epilogue

Maybe my talk may end here. in describing/shaping you and making you realize how much valuable you're and how much capable you're in achieving your goals.

No words can match you exactly, to describe you wholly.

- **You're better than you think**
- **More realistic than you act and**
- **More knowledgeable than you learn.**

Don't stop. it's not your end.

know that life is a one-time invitation, let the whole world should celebrate your success on one day, that you feel you will get your one day on someday.

STAY POSITIVE

BE HOPEFUL &

KEEP GOING...

I believe in you. You will succeed, don't deny whatever things you're pursuing to succeed.

I couldn't stop writing, because you shouldn't lose your confidence after logging out of this book.

KEEP THIS BOOK SAFELY, TO FIND YOU HERE, WHEN YOU ARE LOST IN THE WORLD.

Printed by Libri Plureos GmbH in Hamburg,
Germany